HOW TO BE A VOICE OVER SUCCESS!

FIND THE
POWER and MONEY
IN YOUR VOICE

HOW TO BE A VOICE OVER SUCCESS!
©2014 Madeleine Wild
Audio CD/Files ℗2007, 2014 Madeleine Wild

Madeleine Wild MA, Radio Magic
Happy Lane, Sonoma, CA 95476
www.radiomagic.com

License Agreement
HOW TO BE A VOICE OVER SUCCESS!
This guide is intended for practice only. Materials and music
may not be used for demos or commercial purposes without
permission from Madeleine Wild.

Special thanks to my family and friends:

Michael Wild Blumenfeld
Jane Carrel
Phil Wild
Roy Blumenfeld
Walter Wild (Dad)
Catherine Sevenau
Heather Piazza
John DeGaetano
Mari Cea
Betsy Rodden

CONTENTS

INTRODUCTION
The Key To Voice Over Success

There's an old Vaudeville joke:
How do you get to Carnegie Hall?
Practice. Practice. Practice.

To perform at this world-class music venue, practice is a necessity. The same applies to voice over success. If you want to excel in the art and skill of voice over, you'll need to be prepared. And that means practicing, building experience and finding your true voice power. So, how do you get there? You need rich content, resources, and guidance from someone who has been successful. Madeleine Wild's book, *How To Be a Voice Over Success*, is a perfect place to start.

It's a fun-filled, learn-by-doing, results-oriented system— with scripts, exercises, voice acting tips and more. The tools and techniques you'll practice will stretch your creative imagination, provide a foundation to discover your unique **vocal personality**, and help you stand out in this competitive field.

Practice the techniques in this guidebook with **free** downloadable audio files, accessible with proof of purchase at www.radiomagic.com. Your audio includes music tracks, location sounds, voice over samples and training tips.

BEFORE YOU BEGIN, A FEW THINGS ABOUT VOICE OVER

- **Voice over is an experience in discovering yourself.**

- **Voice over is more than just having a good sounding voice.** It's about music, color, texture, rhythm and timing.

- **Your voice is unique, like a personal signature.** Finding your true voice can help express who you are. Call it the OM, the honey, the hum, the music and the tone you project... Through practice and training you'll discover and define your special qualities.

- **Doing a voice over is like taking snapshots.** "Take one, take two..." Try different angles/poses using your voice until you choose the right one.

- **How many ways can you say it?** There is no single way to read copy. There is no right way. The style changes with the choices we make.

- **The art of voice over acting is in the details.** Practice, observe human qualities and apply them in your narrations and character portrayals. Use body language to express and imagine the character. Pay attention to details and you will bring life to your performance.

- **To become an effective voice actor, you must be real and believable.** Avoid sounding like you're "reading" a script or trying to imitate someone doing a professional commercial on the radio or TV. Don't read for the sake of it, but for the sense of it! Learn how to express yourself in a natural, authentic voice.

PART ONE
Introducing The Voice Over Toolbox

It's not just the sound of your voice. It involves much more. Voice over is an art and a skill. Like all art, it's important to express a point of view, attitude and style in order to be effective. With these intentions in mind, how do you get there? The *Voice Over Toolbox* provides the way. Think of it as the vehicle, the lens, or the roadmap to the power of your voice. Designed to act as your *personal coach,* it's a collection of sensory, visual and imaginary tools to guide you to read scripts and communicate with purpose, focus and clarity.

The *Voice Over Toolbox* includes *Creative* and *Technical* tools. In the end, both work together to prepare you to read effectively, deliver credible characters, and make the words come alive. You'll learn how to:

- Read lines to make them sound natural and conversational.
- Find the rhythm and timing, pace and tone in those words.
- Choose what to emphasize, and how to enunciate, without sounding affected.

Practice using your *Creative* and *Technical* tools along with listening to the *MP3 Audio Download.* In the process, you'll polish your skills, gain confidence and define your *vocal personality.*

Creative Tools: MUSIC (tracks 2-9)

"If you're musically inclined, you have an instinctive sense of the music of speech."
-Will Ryan, Voice Actor, *I Know That Voice* (movie trailer)

Add music to your practice workouts. Music is a guide to creating, defining and maintaining a character and style. Music puts you in a groove and keeps you there.

On the *MP3 Audio Download* you'll hear voice over samples with different music backgrounds. Following, are a variety of music tracks, each approximately timed at 30-seconds, to accompany your reads. Halfway through playing the music you will hear the sound of a bell ("ding") to let you know that you are at the 15-second mark.

Choose a musical style to help you feel a particular mood (but don't *sing* it). Just let the music inspire you as you hear it in the background, and place your voice into a context.

Listen to the *Music* introduction (track 2) and the timed music tracks on the *MP3 Audio Download*:

- Jazz (track 3)
- Country (track 4)
- Classical (track 5)
- Magical (track 6)
- Latin (track 7)
- Business (track 8)
- Dramatic, Intense (track 9)

Music and voice over are truly harmonious art forms. Here are more comments from celebrity voice actors and one elementary school student who might agree with this idea:

"I approach voice over as music."
-Jess Harnell, Voice Actor, *I Know That Voice* (movie trailer)

"Every character has a rhythm."
-Billy West, Voice Actor, *I Know That Voice* (movie trailer)

"I've got the words, now I have to get the music into them."
-Comments from a young student writing a poem. Lucy Calkins, Author, Educator, *The Reading and Writing Project*.

Note:
While music is a powerful and effective way to practice, don't necessarily expect to hear a music accompaniment at your next audition or voice over job. Producers usually add their music later. However, applying the *Voice Over Toolbox* music technique, you should be able to recall a variety of music styles from your practice experiences. Be inspired by simply imagining the rhythm, pace and feeling of a music style, *i.e., jazz, country, classical...* to help maintain any desired style/attitude.

Creative Tools: ATTITUDES (track 10)

Do people say you have a great voice? Success in voice over is not just about the *sound* of your voice; it's how you use it. Expressing an *attitude* is a powerful way to guide you in defining a character, style or point of view. Your *attitude* may be happy, friendly, wacky, or serious... There are endless possibilities when it comes to tapping into our human emotions. Here are a variety of *attitudes* for you to draw on when reading your scripts:

1. friendly
2. happy
3. sad
4. angry
5. fearful
6. playful
7. monotone
8. cool / hip
9. dramatic
10. child-like
11. shy
12. seductive
13. flirty
14. surprised
15. scared / fearful
16. nerdy
17. informative
18. ditsy

19 . tough / pushy

20 . business-like

21 . sarcastic

22 . outdoorsy

23 . motherly / fatherly

24 . grandparent-like

25 . talking to children

26 . teacher-like

27 . gossipy

28 . flamboyant / showy

29 . superior / snobby

30 . know-it-all

31 . whiny / complaining

32 . secretive

33 . intelligent / academic

34 . honest

35 . real / natural

36 . excited

37 . upbeat

38 . spacey / airy

39 . contemporary

40 . wry

41 . authoritative

42 . relaxed

43 . suave / smooth

44 . exotic

45 . magical

46. romantic

Are there other attitudes can you think of?

Listen to *Attitudes* (track 10) with coaching tips and voice acting examples on the *MP3 Audio Download*.

Creative Tools: COLORS (track 11)

Colors act as sensory vehicles to different attitudes. By visualizing a color when reading the copy aloud, it can help to create and maintain a mood or feeling through the tone of your voice.

As you read a commercial, narration or a script, you'll discover *colorful* ways to develop characters and express your *vocal personality* and style.

Listen to the *MP3 Audio Download*

- Does *yellow* make you feel bright and sunny?

- Does *red* represent energy, excitement or anger?

- Is *blue* cool and calming?

- Is *brown* earthy and tough?

Besides the variety of colors in the *Color Toolbox*, you can choose to use different *intensities* and *shades* of the same color.

For example, you could *immerse yourself* in a particular color or apply a *soft brush stroke*.

Let's take the color, RED. As you vocalize the following one-liner, say it with high energy:

WOW! I CAN'T BELIEVE IT!!

Now, try applying a *soft brush stroke* as you say the same one-liner softly, but still with some *red energy* and enthusiasm:

Wow. I can't believe it.

Paint a picture with words using colors! Notice as your color choices change, so will the sound, tone and style of your voice.

Here are your *Colors*:

Red - Energy, vitality, fun

Orange - Warm, smooth, some energy, nurturing

Yellow - Bright, sunny, clear, gentle

Green - Fresh, alive, invigorating, natural, outdoorsy

Blue - Cool, calming, fluid, and poetic

Pink - Airy, lacy, soft, feminine

Violet - Rich, sensory

Grey - Business-like, intelligent, serious

Brown - Earthy, masculine, tough, gritty

Black - Monotone, straightforward, serious, cold, ominous

Silver - Classy

Listen to *Colors* (track 11) with coaching tips and voice acting examples on the *MP3 Audio Download*.

Creative Tools: **CAREERS** (track 12)

Identifying with a career or profession can help you find the right voice. As you vocalize a script, imagine, from inside/out and head to toe, that you are *living* your role. And once you do, you must be able to maintain that character, personality and style, from beginning to end.

Consider factors such as accents, dialects, style, age, gender and size. Be inspired by a well-known celebrity you've seen on TV or in the movies. Try to think of a family member, friend, classmate, business associate, or a hero from a book. Sometimes looking at a picture or a drawing of an animated character can help in creating the perfect voice.

Imagine "dressing" for the part. What would the character wear? Is it something casual or formal? What kind of voice suits their particular career and unique personality? The more specific you can be, the better.

For example, let's say you are a:

• Movie Star - *But, what kind of movie star are you? Intense? Striking and dazzling? Or, down to earth?*

• Cab Driver - *But, what kind of cab driver are you? Tough and jaded? Or, friendly and helpful?*

• Teacher - *But, what kind of teacher are you? Strict or easy-going? Engaging or boring?*

Visualize and define your character in as much detail as possible—and the voice will follow.

Try this exercise: Choose a career, profession or character from the list below. Become the voice of a:

- Computer Geek
- Game Show Host
- Movie Star
- Waiter
- Chef
- Secret agent
- Corporate President
- Boss (Employer)
- Doctor
- Teacher
- Artist
- Explorer
- Farmer
- Dog walker
- Gardener
- Student
- Writer
- Space Alien
- Yoga Practitioner
- Musician
- Sales Person
- Scientist
- Athlete
- Newscaster
- Skydiver
- Magician
- Teen Skateboarder
- Parent
- Grandparent
- Cab driver

Can you think of other careers, professions and characters?

Listen to *Careers* (track 12) with coaching tips and voice acting examples on the *MP3 Audio Download*.

Creative Tools: LOCATION SOUNDS (tracks 13 -20)

Consider the following contexts and visualize:

Where are you... in the city, country, or at the beach?

What is the weather... is it a rainy, snowy or bright and sunny?

Are you indoors... sleeping in bed, cooking in the kitchen, talking on the phone?

Are you outdoors... driving, gardening, fishing, skiing, or swimming?

Are you in a public setting... in a crowd, an auditorium, theater, at a music or sports event, or at the grocery store?

Are you in a small, private setting... at a cozy restaurant, slow dancing or in a sauna?

Are you at a casual or a formal event... at a friendly neighborhood gathering, a graduation, or a wedding?

Add *Location Sounds* to help place your voice into a context, situation or setting. Where are you? Are you in a happy, wild or somber setting? Let your voice convey a tone that fits into a particular location and *be there*. You can also imagine "dressing" your character to suit the occasion and setting.

Try using *Location Sounds* as backgrounds for a variety of scripts in PART TWO.

Listen to *Location Sounds* (track 13) with coaching tips and the following sound backgrounds on the *MP3 Audio Download*

- City (track 14)
- Country (track 15)
- Beach (track 16)
- Restaurant (track 17)
- Office (track 18)
- Airport (track 19)
- Space (track 20)

Can you imagine your voice in other locations?

Creative Tools: BODY LANGUAGE

When you do a voice over, even though you're the "unseen" person behind the microphone, you can use your eyes, hands, facial expressions and stance to make the words come alive. Smile and we can hear it!

Here are examples of how *body language* can help convey emotions with different *attitudes* using the same word:

Try using your body language as you say the word, "NO" in 3 different ways:

FEAR: *Put your hands on your face and scream,* **"NOooo!"**

ANXIETY: *Close your eyes, make a grimace and say,* **"NO..."**

JOY: *Smiling, you can't believe the good news. Say,* **"No!!"**

Stand in front of a mirror to practice using body language.
When you're interpreting a script, commercial, narration, or making a presentation, don't just read it. Picture yourself talking to someone and make it sound believable. Now, try talking on the phone in front of a mirror and observe your natural gestures as you speak to the person on the receiving end. You will feel and hear the difference!

Strike a pose.
Use *body language* to convey and express emotions. Allow yourself to FEEL what you're saying. Be natural, animated, and human. Express yourself!

Creative Tools: CREATING ANIMATED CHARACTERS

Even though animated characters may not be real, you'll still want to portray them as if they were. You can make an inanimate object sound genuine, sincere, menacing... Strive to make these imaginary characters sound authentic and your audience will believe it.

Start by imagining your character from head to toe, inside/out. In addition, it's useful to see a drawing, picture, puppet or model representing your character. It might be helpful to do an online search to better understand your character. Once, I had to portray a parrot for a children's CD-ROM. To find the perfect voice, I researched the web for real life parrots and listened to the way they sounded. Another time, I played a chicken for a children's CD-ROM game. During the recording session we decided it was better to say, "buck, buck, buck" instead of "cluck, cluck, cluck." These small details matter.

Find the right voice for your character.
Consider the way you carry yourself, your posture, head, face and *body language*. Where is the voice originating and from what part of your body? Is it the head, chest, or belly? All affect the tone of your voice and delivery. Whatever you choose, free yourself to be true to your character. Try not to feel self-conscious. Be spontaneous and improvisational. You (and your clients) will be amazed at how you'll bring that character to life.

Try this exercise: **You're a cat. How many ways can you say, "Meow"**
Depending on the character of the cat, your "Meow," may sound sweet, purring, quiet (almost inaudible), screeching, demanding, whining, pissed off... and it will reveal your cat's personality and attitude.

Technical Tools: BASICS

Remember to breathe!

Shallow, nervous breathing can make your voice lack resonance and sound weak. Before reading aloud, breathe slowly, in and out several times. You might even yawn, too, as a way to relax. Breathing deeply and naturally is grounding, like the roots of a tree. The simple act of breathing, and being mindful of good posture, can dramatically improve the quality of your voice. Practice this and you'll discover a fuller, richer, more clear and polished sound. Amazing!

Find ways to make sense out of the copy.

It is essential to read for meaning and understanding. If you don't get it, your audience certainly will not. Use your voice to communicate. Coach yourself into finding the meaning and sense of the copy. As you read through a script, become your own inner voice coach. Try asking some of these questions: "who," "what," "when," "why," "where," and "how."

Making mistakes, like tripping on, mispronouncing or omitting words, are not uncommon and, in fact, come with the territory.

Don't be too hard on yourself! Accept the fact that occasionally making mistakes can be an opportunity to learn and grow. Keep practicing and you'll gain confidence along the way. Think of the ice skaters at the Olympics. What do they do when they trip or fall? They get right back up and continue to skate, without missing a beat! While watching these skaters perform, the viewing audience may anticipate that the Olympic skater will trip or fall. But, when a performer is totally focused, the audience can enjoy the show and not worry that the skater will fall. The same concept is true for voice over actors. When performers are confident and focused in the moment, they are more likely to succeed.

Technical Tools: VOLUME, PITCH AND TONE

Volume: loud and soft
Try reading the same word, raising or lowering your volume, to vary your delivery. Bring it up/down to increase or decrease the intensity of your reading:

HEY!!!	*Loud, big, projecting, out there voice*
Hey.	*Soft, light, airy, personal, intimate voice*

Here are more ways to *place your voice* in proximity to your audience. Practice reading the same one-liner aloud and try using a different volume (or "distance") for the same line in the following contexts — *a whisper, an audible whisper, across the table, across the room, and across the street*. How many ways can you say the following one-liner?

Good morning. How are you?

- *A whisper* – You are telling a secret. It's really soft. A total whisper.

- *An audible whisper* – You're speaking quietly into a lover's ear or to a friend late at night on the phone.

- *Across the table* – You're having a meal at home or in a restaurant and are talking naturally, in a moderate tone.

- *Across the room* – You are starting to project your voice a bit.

- *Across the street (or across a football field)* – You're really projecting, so that your neighbor across the street can hear you. Or, a teammate can hear you across the football field.

Consider the pitch of your voice

Pitch represents the ups and downs of your voice. It's the musical level at which you speak. Is the pitch high or low? These subtleties affect the *attitude* and help define the character and style of your vocal delivery.

Read the same line twice, in a *high* and *low pitch*.

What a surprise!	*Say this line in a higher pitch*
What a surprise.	*Say this line in a lower pitch*

Tone is the sound quality of your voice

You can be warm, rich, soft, sexy, raspy, tough, playful, smooth, authoritative and more. The tone(s) you project can be an important key to your voice over success! Call it the *OM*, the *honey*, and the *music* in your voice that attracts attention.

Vary the tone of your voice, depending on your audience and creative intentions. To whom are you speaking? Before reading a script, consider the age, gender, and size of your audience. If you're doing a voice over for kids, teens, parents, romantic couples, sports enthusiasts, educators, business people or elders, you'll want to use the appropriate tone of voice.

Like a musician or singer perfecting their sounds, you can cultivate your tonal quality through practice and awareness. Tone of voice communicates volumes and represents your unique *vocal personality*. Use it to your advantage and your audience will *hear* the difference!

Technical Tools: TIME, TIMING, TEMPO AND PAUSES

Keeping time

Read aloud along with the timed music selections to keep track of your time. After much practice, professionals will often say that they develop an *inner clock* sense of time. They can easily gauge what constitutes a 15-second, 30-second or 60-second commercial spot. Timing your reads can take your mind off "thinking too much" and instead, keep you focused.

Timing is everything!

Timing is different from keeping time. It is the use of rhythm, tempo and pausing to enhance comedy, humor and meaning. The pacing of the delivery of a line can have a strong impact on its effect, even altering its meaning.

Tempo and Pace refers to the speed of your voice and the accompanying music.

Is the tempo of your voice too fast, too slow, or is it just right for the copy? When you deliver a line, you would not want to rush a romantic piece of copy, but you might want to read the announcer tag more quickly. The voice over for an audio book or a museum audio guide would require a different tempo than reading a 30-second commercial. It all depends on the script. Whatever it is, make sure to maintain a consistent pace throughout.

It's what you don't hear that speaks volumes...

With voice over, singing and music, the unheard words and pauses can sometimes be the most powerful. When you're delivering a speech, recording a voice over, or narrating a story, find the natural pauses. Take a beat... we do it all the time in real conversation.

Technical Tools: MARKING THE COPY

Mark the copy to create a road map when reading copy. Underline or highlight the written page to help guide you in choosing emphasis and timing. Choreograph which words you want to emphasize, where to pause or breathe, and mark places for sending your tone *up, across* or *down*. Mark your trouble words, the ones you're likely to slip up on.

Here are examples for *marking the copy* in the following one-liner:

It's the best choice you can make.

/   *Pause or breath:* It's the best choice/ you can make.

//   *Two beats pause or breath:* It's the best choice// you can make.

///   *Three beats pause or breath:* It's the best choice/// you can make.

//// *Long pause or breath:* It's the best choice//// you can make.

Equal emphasis: It's <u>the</u> <u>best</u> choice you can make.

Double underline for accent: It's the <u>best</u> choice you can make.

Emphasis is UP: It's the best choice you can <u>make</u>. ^

Emphasis is ACROSS: It's the best choice you can <u>make</u>. >

Emphasis is DOWN: It's the best choice you can <u>make</u>. v

Attitude/Style: Mark as *friendly, business-like, sultry...*

Pacing: Mark the copy as *fast, slow...*

Draw parentheses or brackets around certain company names, commercial sponsors, addresses, phone numbers or important information, slogans and phrases that you'll want to remember, so that you'll read that portion of the copy smoothly as one idea. For example, here are one-liners from commercials:

Before marking the copy:

Come to the All-You–Can-Eat Fresh Fruit and Salad Bar at Denny's.

After marking the copy:

Come to (the All–You-Can-Eat) (Fresh Fruit and Salad Bar) at Denny's.

Here are more examples of marking the copy:

- Call and ask about our (Toyota Spring Special Tune-Up) today.

- (Taylor Maid Farms/Organic Coffee & Tea.) (It's fair trade certified) and (one hundred percent organic.)

- To place your order call (The Red Grape Restaurant) at (707-996-4444)

Marking the copy is a good way to plan your direction, gain confidence and make sense out of reading any script.

Technical Tools: PUNCTUATION, ENUNCIATION, AND CLARITY

Take advantage of periods and acknowledge punctuation.
Periods and commas are like *stop signs*. A period provides a structure — a refreshing *pause* or a *beat* — to think and convey meaning. Try not to ignore those periods. Some people are reluctant to pause, afraid of those empty spaces. Pausing for a beat may even seem like an eternity, but it's not necessarily as long as you may imagine.

When reading copy, be aware of commas and periods, and pause for a beat or two. This helps with rhythm, timing and pacing. You can mark the copy like this: Count the beats with visual notations like these: / // /// or more, depending on the nature of the script. Commercial copy usually requires fewer beats; narrations tend to have longer pauses.

To enunciate or not... that is the question.
Enunciation is especially important in certain more formal contexts when you are reading for narration, spokesperson, technical, industrial, and education purposes. Try not to slide words into each other. It's essential to pronounce words clearly and precisely from beginning to end and to enunciate with clarity. At the same time, those words must sound smooth, natural, and be effortlessly executed.

However, for certain commercials, animation, characters and real person (conversational) contexts, slang is okay for authenticity. In fact, *real* and *natural* are very important styles you'll want to master.

Read the same line in two different ways:

I'm outta here	I'm out of here
He's sitting innis car	He's sitting in his car
The bird is inner nest	The bird is in her nest
Here's ta the crazy ones	Here's to the crazy ones
I'm ready fer anything	I'm ready for anything

To enunciate or not… One is slang; the other is not. Be aware of the difference and prepared to perform either way.

Speak with clarity
It's important to speak clearly and to pronounce words *from beginning to end*. At the same time, those words must sound smooth, connected and believable. The following are most commonly mispronounced. Pay special attention to enunciating words, such as:

- "to," instead of "ta" For the perfect sounding "to" think of the number "2"

- "for," instead of "fer" For the perfect sounding "for" think of the number "4"

- Pronounce endings of words, such as "and," instead of "an."

- Don't overemphasize. Lightly tap the "d" in "and"

- Don't let endings of sentences drop off unintentionally.

- Avoid popping the "Ps" and "Bs." In the studio these can come across as a distracting sound.

Technical Tools: EMPHASIS AND PHRASING

Some people have a natural ability to group words and read phrases. Sometimes a reader may put the emphasis on words in questionable places that do not make sense. Think about how you would emphasize the following words:

- Recording studio
- Bird house
- Air filter

Your answer: Emphasis is on the first word. Try putting the emphasis on the second word and see how odd these common phrases sound.

Here are more examples:

Join us in the living <u>room</u>.

Join us in the <u>living</u> room.
This is the correct emphasis

The people of earth now travel <u>between</u> the stars.

The people of earth now travel between the <u>stars</u>.
This is the correct emphasis

As you read copy, more often than not, you should emphasize the action word over the Personal Pronoun.

Personal Pronouns

I	we
you	you (plural)
he she, it	they

Action Words VS Personal Pronouns

Action Words are verbs. Here are examples of action words from the copy below: *play, jump, love.*

Try reading the following one-liners in different ways.
Hear the difference it makes when you emphasize the *Action Word* instead of the *Personal Pronoun*:

Example 1

Are <u>we</u> ready to play?	*Emphasize the Personal Pronoun*
Are we ready to <u>play</u>?	*Emphasize the Action Word*

Example 2

<u>You</u> can jump on board!	*Emphasize the Personal Pronoun*
You can <u>jump</u> on board!	*Emphasize the Action Word*

Example 3

<u>I</u> love them!	*Emphasize the Personal Pronoun*
I <u>love</u> them!	*Emphasize the Action Word*

Color the words and make them come alive!

Speak words and convey an emotion in a way that corresponds to the word's meaning. Sometimes this is called, *coloring the words*. For example: *warm* is spoken warmly; *happy* can be said with a smile, and *sad* with a frown. When words are spoken with *a sensory picture in mind*, the speaker and listener are able to visualize, connect to them and construct a clear picture of the meaning.

S-t-r-e-t-c-h a word!

Think of a word as a piece of clay in your hands. You can roll it, bounce it, throw it, squish it and stretch it. Say it fast. Now say it slowly. Press the palms of your hands together and imagine you are holding the word between your hands. Now, slowly pull your hands apart, making the space between them bigger. As you progress, continuing to slowly stretch it out, you'll hear the *sound* of your word expand. This is similar to a singer or musician holding a musical note.

Try this technique with the following words:
sweet
love
beautiful
oh
surprise

Technical Tools: TAKING CARE OF YOUR VOICE FOR OPTIMUM PERFORMANCE

Do's and Don'ts for recording, auditions and public speaking

Keep your voice in good shape and it will take care of you. Before you read or are ready to audition, here are a few suggestions for physically fine tuning and enhancing the quality of your voice:

- *Water is key!* Room temperature water, warm water with or without honey/lemon, or bottled water, are good things to have on hand. They also help lubricate and relax the throat, especially if you have a sore throat or raspy voice. Stay hydrated in preparation for a session and throughout the day.

- *Thayer's Dry Mouth Spray and Slippery Elm Lozenges, Biotene, dental gum and eating a green apple* can be remedies for dry mouth and unwanted mouth sounds. They help relax, soothe the throat, and reduce unwanted sounds, like clicking or smacking.

- *Avoid smoking, coffee, alcohol, and spicy foods.* Try not to smoke or consume coffee, alcohol, and spicy foods a few hours before or during a recording session. They can be dehydrating.

- *Avoid eating dairy products* since they are mucous producing. Eliminating these foods prior to a session can help reduce "throat clearing" during a session.

PART TWO
Getting Started

This is where you'll have the chance to put the *Creative* and *Technical* tools from PART ONE into practice! You'll read scripts, drawing from your *Voice Over Toolbox*, to create styles, characters, and improve technical skills.

There are a variety of timed scripts for you to explore. one-liners, 15-second, 30–second and 60-second scripts.

Before you begin to read each script, look at the heading and consider who's talking (*Announcer, Narrator, Character, Spokesperson or Real Person*). Make a choice. Then, experiment with other voice options.

How many ways can you read each script? First, follow the director's choice from the *Creative Tools (Music, Attitudes, Colors, Careers and Location Sounds,* located under each script. Then, choose the styles you want to explore. Hear the difference as your choices change. Have fun and play with the possibilities!

Choose Music Tracks and Location Sounds on the *MP3 Audio Download* to accompany your voice as you read the scripts. Record yourself, play it back and critique your performance. Try different ways each time. Listen to coaching tips, voice over examples, timed Music Tracks, Attitudes, Colors, Careers, and Location Sounds.

AUDIO GUIDE

Here is the playlist for the MP3 Audio Download:

1.	Let's Get Started	
2.	**Music**	1:25
3.	Jazz	0:30
4.	Country	0:30
5.	Classical	0:30
6.	Magical	0:30
7.	Latin	0:30
8.	Business	0:30
9.	Dramatic	0:30
10.	**Attitudes**	1:25
11.	**Colors**	1:04
12.	**Careers**	0:42
13.	**Location Sounds**	0:30
14.	City	0:30
15.	Country	0:30
16.	Beach	0:30
17.	Restaurant	0:30
18.	Office	0:30
19.	Airport	0:30
20.	Space	0:30

Listen to the *MP3 Audio Download,* which includes: Music Tracks, Location Sounds, and Training Tips and Techniques from the *Voice Over Toolbox:*

- Coaching tips
- Voice over examples
- Music tracks
- Location sounds
        And more…

34

On the *MP3 Audio Download*, you'll hear my coaching tips, along the following voice examples (and more), demonstrating techniques from the *Voice Over Toolbox*:

Music (tracks 2,3,4) "Listen to the voice say the following lines in three different musical backgrounds: *jazz, country, classical.*"

Attitudes (track 10) "Listen to the voice say the following lines in three different attitudes: *warm, secretive, excited.*"

Colors (track 11) "Listen to the voice say the following lines in four different colors: *yellow, red, brown, pink.*"

Location Sounds (track 13) "Listen to the sounds and atmospheres to help place your voice into a context when reading your lines."

CREATING A PLAN FOR YOUR PRACTICE WORKOUTS

Customize your workouts.
First, practice, one at a time, with each of the *Creative* tools from the *Voice Over Toolbox*. Then add and combine other tools and techniques to the practice session. Read scripts along with your choice of music tracks and location sounds from the *MP3 Audio Download*. Try to deliver your reads in the timeframe allotted for the spot. Record yourself and gauge your improvement.

The *Voice Over Toolbox* is designed to provide a foundation for reading *any* script, no matter what the content. Practice takes commitment and using these techniques can be entertaining and serious fun!

How much time should you set aside for practice?
I recommend 10-30 minutes or more per day. Or, try practicing every other day, once or twice a week... whatever fits into your life. Just do the best you can to commit to a practice schedule that will bring results. Know that the more you practice, the more confident you'll become.

You can enrich your practice and training by simply listening and tuning into the world around you.
For inspiration, listen to and observe radio/TV/film performers as well as everyday people in your life. Wherever you are — at a park, standing in line at the market, at a party or event, talking on the phone — notice the way people express themselves. Be aware of their body language, voice characteristics, accents, dialects and idiosyncrasies. Store observations in your "memory bank" so that you can draw from these real life human qualities when you create a character or style.

ONE-LINER WARM UPS

Directions for reading one-liners with the Voice Over Toolbox

As you read through the one-liners, choose a music track or location sound from the *MP3 Audio Download* for the entire 32 lines; then try others for the next read. Attitudes, Colors and Careers may also be combined during your one-liner exercises.

- Hello, anybody out there?
- Who do you think you are?
- It's time to go.
- I don't believe it.
- Sorry, wrong number.
- What did you say?
- Yes.
- No.
- Oh.
- Why?
- Stop.
- Go.
- Help.
- Wow.
- I need you.
- You'll never get away with this!
- I want more.

- I'm shocked. This has got to be a dream!
- Feels like velvet.
- Tastes good.
- Look at the rainbow.
- Did you hear that?
- You're crazy.
- You can do it.
- I'll never forget that.
- It's icy cold.
- The wind is so strong today.
- It's raining.
- Get out of the water.
- Please don't cry.
- You're so adorable.
- That is hilarious.

MUSIC *track 2*
Take one: jazz - track 3
Take two: dramatic - track 9
Take three: Latin - track 7

ATTITUDES *track 10*
Take one: happy
Take two: business-like
Take three: excited

COLORS *track 11*
Take one: red
Take two: pink
Take three: brown

CAREERS *track 12*
Take one: doctor
Take two: movie star
Take three: secret agent

LOCATION SOUNDS *track 13*
Take one: city - track 14
Take two: country - track 15
Take three: beach - track 16

FIFTEEN-SECOND SCRIPTS

1. Commercial - The Future of Energy - Announcer, Spokesperson, Character

Ladies and Gentleman: Introducing THE SUN. Now, for the first time in history, the energy of the sun can be brought to your home for a very affordable price.

MUSIC *track 2*
Take one: jazz - track 3
Take two: country - track 4
Take three: classical - track 5

ATTITUDES *track 10*
Take one: warm
Take two: secretive
Take three: excited

COLORS *track 11*
Take one: yellow
Take two: red
Take three: grey

CAREERS *track 12*
Take one: scientist
Take two: teacher
Take three: game show host

LOCATION SOUNDS *track 13*
Take one: city - track 14
Take two: office - track 18
Take three: space - track 20

2. Commercial - Sound Soother - Announcer, Real Person

Life is something that happens when you can't get to sleep. Consider these sleep tips from the experts: read a book, drink warm milk and get the Sound Soother, a portable white-noise machine. Call (800) 344-4444

MUSIC *track 2*
Take one: magical - track 6
Take two: classical - track 5
Take three: jazz - track 3

ATTITUDES *track 10*
Take one: motherly/fatherly
Take two: relaxed
Take three: monotone

COLORS *track 11*
Take one: orange
Take two: pink
Take three: violet

CAREERS *track 12*
Take one: doctor
Take two: scientist
Take three: sales person

LOCATION SOUNDS *track 13*
Take one: beach - track 16
Take two: city - track 14
Take three: space - track 20

3. Commercial - Hair Product - Announcer, Real Person

Go ahead. Touch it. Wild, sexy hair. Take a walk on the wild side. This new WILD line of products brings fun and style into one. Take long, short, curly, or straight hair from bland to wild instantly. 100% percent fun and flirty.

MUSIC track 2
Take one: jazz - track 3
Take two: magical - track 6
Take three: Latin - track 7

ATTITUDES track 10
Take one: flirty
Take two: cool
Take three: hip

COLORS track 11
Take one: red
Take two: violet
Take three: pink

CAREERS track 12
Take one: movie star
Take two: gossip
Take three: sales person

LOCATION SOUNDS track 13
Take one: city - track 14
Take two: restaurant - track 18
Take three: office - track 20

4. Commercial - Honda Insight - Announcer, Spokesperson, Real Person

Imagine a new kind of car — environmentally conscious with extraordinary technology to achieve the best gas mileage in America. Sleek, sporty, and of course, very affordable. Now, imagine a cleaner world. The Honda Insight. No longer a figment of your imagination.

MUSIC *track 2*
Take one: jazz - track 3
Take two: dramatic - track 9
Take three: classical - track 5

ATTITUDES *track 10*
Take one: relaxed
Take two: intelligent
Take three: upbeat

COLORS *track 11*
Take one: blue
Take two: grey
Take three: green

CAREERS *track 12*
Take one: scientist
Take two: newscaster
Take three: corporate president

LOCATION SOUNDS *track 13*
Take one: city - track 14
Take two: space - track 20
Take three: beach - track 16

5. Commercial - Country Hearth Bread - Announcer, Real person

Very early in the morning Country Hearth begins baking bread. They use the same ingredients you'd use, if you were baking bread for your own family. Country fresh eggs, pure vegetable shortening, quality-enriched flour, never any preservatives.

MUSIC track 2
Take one: classical - track 5
Take two: magical - track 6
Take three: country - track 4

ATTITUDES track 10
Take one: warm
Take two: relaxed
Take three: talking to children

COLORS track 11
Take one: yellow
Take two: orange
Take three: brown

CAREERS track 12
Take one: grandparent
Take two: teacher
Take three: farmer

LOCATION SOUNDS track 13
Take one: country – track 15
Take two: office - track 18
Take three: space - track 20
Take three: space track 20

6. Commercial - National Hot Dog Month - Character, Announcer

This is National Hot Dog Month, National Hot Dog Month - a time to recognize and re-evaluate the hot dog. Complete with bun, mustard, chili, cheese, onion, pickle and sauerkraut.

MUSIC track 2
Take one: country - track 4
Take two: jazz - track 3
Take three: classical - track 5

ATTITUDES track 10
Take one: happy
Take two: authoritative
Take three: cool, hip

COLORS track 11
Take one: red
Take two: black
Take three: green

CAREERS track 12
Take one: farmer
Take two: cab driver
Take three: chef

LOCATION SOUNDS track 13
Take one: city - track 14
Take two: country - track 15
Take three: office - track 20

7. Commercial - Supermarket - Animated Character

As Head Lettuce, I hereby call to order this meeting of the Vegetable Council. It's come to our attention that certain vegetables are slacking off, like the tomatoes.

MUSIC *track 2*
Take one: magical - track 6
Take two: dramatic - track 9
Take three: country - track 4

ATTITUDES *track 10*
Take one: nerdy
Take two: flamboyant, showy
Take three: playful

COLORS *track 11*
Take one: red
Take two: brown
Take three: grey

CAREERS *track 12*
Take one: boss (employer)
Take two: musician
Take three: game show host

LOCATION SOUNDS *track 13*
Take one: country - track 15
Take two: restaurant - track 17
Take three: office - track 18

8. Kids' CD-ROM - "Orly's Draw-A-Story" - Character

Hey! That's my planet down there. What are you doing in outer space? In bug language we call our planet Jebubblenexertroff. Look, I'm floating! This is great!

MUSIC *track 2*
Take one: magical - track 6
Take two: country - track 4
Take three: classical - track 5

ATTITUDES *track 10*
Take one: playful
Take two: secretive
Take three: tough, pushy

COLORS *track 11*
Take one: yellow
Take two: red
Take three: pink

CAREERS *track 12*
Take one: explorer
Take two: magician
Take three: teen skateboarder

LOCATION SOUNDS *track 13*
Take one: beach - track 16
Take two: country - track 15
Take three: space - track 20

9. Fairytale Storybook - "The Frog Prince" - Narrator, Character

The prince looked at the princess who had believed him when no one else in the world had, the princess who actually kissed his slimy frog lips. The prince kissed the princess. They both turned into frogs. And they hopped off happily ever after.

MUSIC *track 2*

Take one: magical - track 6
Take two: country - track 4
Take three: classical - track 5

ATTITUDES *track 10*
Take one: happy
Take two: playful
Take three: talking to children

COLORS *track 11*
Take one: yellow
Take two: red
Take three: pink

CAREERS *track 12*
Take one: entertainer
Take two: teacher
Take three: game show host

LOCATION SOUNDS *track 13*
Take one: country - track 15
Take two: beach – track 16
Take three: space - track 20

10. Commercial - Cup of Water - Character

Hi, I'm a cup of water.

Nothing out of the ordinary,

just your average mug of H20.

I like to sit around and not do much of anything.

Uh oh, looks like I'm going into the microwave.

Ohhh, that's hot!

I'm one hot cup of water.

MUSIC *track 2*
Take one: jazz - track 3
Take two: country - track 4
Take three: classical - track 5

ATTITUDES *track 10*
Take one: seductive
Take two: secretive
Take three: cool, hip

COLORS *track 11*
Take one: yellow
Take two: red
Take three: pink

CAREERS *track 12*
Take one: yoga practitioner
Take two: entertainer
Take three: sales person

LOCATION SOUNDS *track 13*
Take one: restaurant - track 17
Take two: office - track 18
Take three: space - track 20

11. Technology - Trade Show - Announcer, Narrator,

Phoenix— the system software at the heart of it all. It's the technology that gives any device its own personality and character. With Phoenix Technology, customers are empowered to optimize their resources, get products to market fast, ensure quality and reliability.

MUSIC *track 2*
Take one: jazz - track 3
Take two: classical - track 5
Take three: business – track 8

ATTITUDES *track 10*
Take one: intelligent
Take two: business-like
Take three: real, natural

COLORS *track 11*
Take one: brown
Take two: blue
Take three: grey

CAREERS *track 12*
Take one: computer geek
Take two: corporate president
Take three: teacher

LOCATION SOUNDS *track 13*
Take one: city - track 14
Take two: office - track 18
Take three: airport - track 19

12. Newscaster - Announcer

And now the News... Could robots begin earning their keep? In Japan, humanoid devices have found work as museum guides, in TV ads, and even in the role of a supermodel. To find out more go to cyborg.com.

MUSIC *track 2*
Take one: business - track 8
Take two: jazz - track 3
Take three: classical - track 5

ATTITUDES *track 10*
Take one: upbeat, friendly
Take two: informative
Take three: excited

COLORS *track 11*
Take one: grey
Take two: red
Take three: blue

CAREERS *track 12*
Take one: newscaster
Take two: teacher
Take three: scientist

LOCATION SOUNDS *track 13*
Take one: city - track 14
Take two: office - track 18
Take three: space - track 20

13. Video Game - "Star Control" - Narrator, Character

It is the year 2155. The people of earth travel between the stars. The future looks bright and full of possibilities. But now, a glorious dream is dashed by the arrival of a hostile armada.

MUSIC *track 2*
Take one: magical - track 6
Take two: dramatic - track 9
Take three: classical - track 5

ATTITUDES *track 10*
Take one: spacey
Take two: dramatic
Take three: monotone

COLORS *track 11*
Take one: black
Take two: blue
Take three: grey

CAREERS *track 12*
Take one: yoga practitioner
Take two: newscaster
Take three: space alien

LOCATION SOUNDS *track 13*
Take one: beach – track 16
Take two: country - track 15
Take three: space - track 20

14. Internet /TV - National Geographic - Announcer, Real Person

Did you ever get the feeling your dog was laughing at you? New research suggests maybe he was! Scientists think those "huffing" noises are doggie laughter. Dogs make them when playing with another animal, person, or just tossing a toy around. Find out more at National Geographic.com.

MUSIC *track 2*
Take one: business - track 8
Take two: country - track 4
Take three: classical - track 5

ATTITUDES *track 10*
Take one: friendly
Take two: scared/fearful
Take three: sarcastic

COLORS *track 11*
Take one: yellow
Take two: red
Take three: orange

CAREERS *track 12*
Take one: writer
Take two: dog walker
Take three: newscaster

LOCATION SOUNDS *track 13*
Take one: city - track 14
Take two: office - track 18
Take three: space - track 20

15. Commercial - Wine Country - Announcer

It's spring in the wine country — the perfect time to visit.
Wineries are un-crowded, back roads open, and rooms
available. Go whale watching, visit historic sites. It's a sure
recipe for a Spring getaway — Sonoma Wine Country. Call for
our free travel brochure.

MUSIC *track 2*
Take one: jazz - track 3
Take two: country - track 4
Take three: classical - track 5

ATTITUDES *track 10*
Take one: warm
Take two: romantic
Take three: upbeat

COLORS *track 11*
Take one: yellow
Take two: violet
Take three: grey

CAREERS *track 12*
Take one: entertainer
Take two: artist
Take three: yoga practitioner

LOCATION SOUNDS *track 13*
Take one: city - track 14
Take two: space - track 20
Take three: beach - track 16

16. Commercial - Wine - Announcer, Real person

Cabernet flavor. Merlot smoothness. The new Gossamer Bay
Merlot Cabernet. It's quite a wine.

MUSIC track 2
Take one: jazz - track 3
Take two: country - track 4
Take three: classical - track 5

ATTITUDES track 10
Take one: warm
Take two: secretive
Take three: seductive

COLORS track 11
Take one: violet
Take two: orange
Take three: grey

CAREERS track 12
Take one: sales person
Take two: entertainer
Take three: waiter

LOCATION SOUNDS track 13
Take one: city - track 14
Take two: country – track 15
Take three: space - track 20

17. Commercial - Potato Chips - Announcer, Real person

It's all about the chips! Before you reach for that sandwich, by all means, get some chips. And not just any chips... Lay's.

MUSIC *track 2*
Take one: country - track 4
Take two: Latin - track 7
Take three: magical - track 6

ATTITUDES *track 10*
Take one: happy
Take two: relaxed
Take three: flirty

COLORS *track 11*
Take one: red
Take two: yellow
Take three: violet

CAREERS *track 12*
Take one: farmer
Take two: sports star
Take three: cab driver

LOCATION SOUNDS *track 13*
Take one: city - track 14
Take two: country - track 15
Take three: airport - track 19

18. Commercial - Sunglasses - Real person

Vectra! There's something about 'em that makes you look better and see better. Or maybe, just maybe, it's the way you feel when you wear 'em. Vectra. Your sunglasses say a lot about you. What do your sunglasses say?

MUSIC *track 2*
Take one: jazz - track 3
Take two: country - track 4
Take three: Latin - track 7

ATTITUDES *track 10*
Take one: seductive
Take two: secretive
Take three: excited

COLORS *track 11*
Take one: yellow
Take two: red
Take three: violet

CAREERS *track 12*
Take one: sports star
Take two: teen skateboarder
Take three: musician

LOCATION SOUNDS *track 13*
Take one: city - track 14
Take two: beach - track 16
Take three: airport – track 19

19. Public Service Announcement (PSA) - E-Waste - Announcer, Spokesperson

Americans discard more than 100 million computers, cellphones, and other electronic devices each year. As "e-waste" piles up, so does concern about the growing threat to the environment. Find out how you can be part of the solution.

MUSIC *track 2*
Take one: jazz - track 3
Take two: dramatic - track 9
Take three: business - track 8

ATTITUDES *track 10*
Take one: real, natural
Take two: intelligent
Take three: honest

COLORS *track 11*
Take one: brown
Take two: red
Take three: grey

CAREERS *track 12*
Take one: scientist
Take two: teacher
Take three: parent

LOCATION SOUNDS *track 13*
Take one: city - track 14
Take two: office - track 18
Take three: space - track 20

20. Online Business - YOU.INC - Announcer, Spokesperson

From an idea of independence to plans to incorporate, each business journey starts with a dream, an inspiration — with people like you. To learn more, visit YOU.INC online at cisco.com.

MUSIC *track 2*
Take one: jazz - track 3
Take two: business - track 8
Take three: classical - track 5

ATTITUDES *track 10*
Take one: upbeat, friendly
Take two: business-like
Take three: cool, hip

COLORS *track 11*
Take one: blue
Take two: red
Take three: grey

CAREERS *track 12*
Take one: parent
Take two: teacher
Take three: newscaster

LOCATION SOUNDS *track 13*
Take one: city - track 14
Take two: office - track 18
Take three: space - track 20

THIRTY-SECOND SCRIPTS

Radio Commercial - Taylor Maid Coffees and Teas - Announcer, Spokesperson

Wake up to a rich, flavorful, shade grown coffee, roasted fresh daily. It's fair trade certified and one hundred percent organic. Relax with an aromatic cup of tea — grown at our beautiful farm and blended with organic herbs and spices from around the world.

Look for Taylor Maid Coffees and Teas at natural food stores and fine cafes.

Visit us online at TaylorMaidFarms.com or call (707) 824-9110.

Enjoy in good conscience.

MUSIC *track 2*
Take one: jazz - track 3
Take two: country - track 4
Take three: classical - track 5

ATTITUDES *track 10*
Take one: warm
Take two: informative
Take three: real, natural

COLORS *track 11*
Take one: yellow
Take two: red
Take three: orange

CAREERS *track 12*
Take one: chef
Take two: explorer
Take three: writer

LOCATION SOUNDS *track 13*
Take one: city - track 14
Take two: office - track 18
Take three: country - track 15

TV Commercial - Waterfresh Water Filters - Real Person, Announcer

It's amazing what some people go through to get fresh drinking water. Especially since there's a much easier way standing right in front of them. It's called a faucet.

With new Waterfresh Water Filters, you can turn your tap water into clean, natural drinking water for less than 25 cents a gallon.

New Waterfresh Water Filters. From Teledyne Water Pik.
It's like bottled water, without the bottle.

MUSIC track 2
Take one: business - track 8
Take two: country - track 4
Take three: classical - track 5

ATTITUDES track 10
Take one: informative
Take two: cool, hip
Take three: real, natural

COLORS track 11
Take one: green
Take two: red
Take three: grey

CAREERS *track 12*
Take one: scientist
Take two: teacher
Take three: yoga practitioner

LOCATION SOUNDS *track 13*
Take one: country - track 15
Take two: beach - track 16
Take three: office - track 18

Radio/TV Commercial - Post Blueberry Morning Cereal - Real Person, Announcer

Remember summer mornings and blueberries so sweet you wanted to put them in a box and enjoy them all year long. That's the taste captured in new Blueberry Morning Cereal. A cereal with real whole blueberries ripened by the summer sun. But more than just blueberries, it's the most delightful mix of light crispy flakes, golden oat clusters and almonds you've ever tasted. It's all there. Taste new Post Blueberry Morning Cereal. A little taste of summer.

MUSIC track 2
Take one: magical - track 6
Take two: country - track 4
Take three: classical - track 5

ATTITUDES track 10
Take one: warm
Take two: real, natural
Take three: upbeat

COLORS track 11
Take one: yellow
Take two: green
Take three: orange

CAREERS track 12
Take one: space alien
Take two: teacher
Take three: gardener

LOCATION SOUNDS track 13
Take one: country - track 15
Take two: office - track 18
Take three: city - track 14

Radio/TV Commercial - Ocean Spray - 1, 2 or more Real Person(s) - *Time it!*

For one, two, or more readers. Attitude is upbeat with energy, and you'll need to come in promptly with your lines. Time it. Can you read this commercial in exactly 30 seconds? This practice will keep you focused and on target.

Voice	:	It's better!
Voice	:	A lot better
Voice	:	Surprise!
Voice	:	Sweet
Voice	:	Mm…Ocean Spray!
Voice	:	Ruby red and tangerine grapefruit juice
Voice	:	This is grapefruit?
Voice	:	It's better
Voice	:	Not bitter
Voice	:	Surprise
Voice	:	Sweet
Voice	:	Good
Voice	:	It has two tastes…
Voice	:	Sweet grapefruit and tangerine
Voice	:	Tangerine?
Voice	:	Wow!
Voice	:	It's better
Voice	:	It's much, much better
Voice	:	Not bitter
Voice	:	What a surprise!
Voice	:	It's very, very sweet
Voice	:	It's not any ordinary grapefruit drink
Voice	:	It's got a sweet taste you'll crave
Voice	:	Ruby red and tangerine
Voice	:	Crave the wave
All:		Ocean spray!

MUSIC *track 2*
Take one: jazz - track 3
Take two: country - track 4
Take three: classical - track 5

ATTITUDES *track 10*
Take one: warm
Take two: secretive
Take three: excited

COLORS *track 11*
Take one: yellow
Take two: red
Take three: grey

CAREERS *track 12*
Take one: scientist
Take two: teacher
Take three: game show host

LOCATION SOUNDS *track 13*
Take one: city - track 14
Take two: office - track 18
Take three: space - track 20

SIXTY-SECOND SCRIPT - Dialog

The following commercial script has two-three parts with suggested directions for reading the script. Try these; then refer to the *Voice Over Toolbox* and choose your own ways.

Announcer:
Choose an attitude:
- Business-like
- Intelligent, academic
- Friendly

Nervous Guy/Gal character:
Choose an attitude:
- Ditsy
- Pushy
- Shy

Imagine this character is talking to:
- An executive
- A board of directors
- A large audience at a conference hall

See script on next page) -->

Radio/TV Commercial - Executive Technique - Character, Announcer

Nervous Guy/Gal: I'd like to present my new invention. Uh, it's this uh, black thing here. You see, with this uh thing, you can talk to someone else. Not that you can't already talk to someone else. But with this you can uh talk to them somewhere else. You put this part on your ear and you talk. Not with your ear, with your mouth, into this part, the receiver. Um, what I mean is, these wires here carry your voice to other wires. I mean, they don't really "carry" it but anyway...

Announcer: Even a brilliant idea can bomb if the presentation isn't equally as impressive. At Executive Technique we've helped Fortune 500 executives in every field sharpen their presentation skills. Our intensive training program includes videotaped practices, and listener critiques so you can develop your own personal style of communication.

Nervous Guy/Gal: Uh, a demonstration? Well, I suppose I'd need another *black thing* to really try it. How about I come back tomorrow?

Announcer: Don't let poor presentation skills get in the way of your company's success. Call the Executive Technique at 1-800-992-1414.

PART THREE
Tracking Your Voice Over Progress

Practice session date:

1. Did you maintain the style or character?

2. Timing/Pacing (too fast, too slow, just right)

3. Was it believable?

4. Did you make *sense* out of the copy?

5. What worked? What did not work?

6. Which styles of Music, Attitudes, Colors, Careers, and Location Sounds did you like working with the best?

7. List intentions for practice and mastering.

Imagine that you are the casting director or client. Evaluate your workout based on each of the questions on the previous page, and add your own notes. Make your own chart!

Rate your performance:

1 - Needs more work

2 - Good

3 - Keeper

Average score:

Use the above critique as a way to build your voice over repertoire, keep track of your progress, and set goals.

DEFINING YOUR PERSONAL STYLE — FINDING THE "MONEY" IN YOUR VOICE!

Your voice is unique, like a personal signature. It has defining qualities, which make it truly yours alone. There are people who have a wide range of voices within, while others have a more singular and focused style. Some prefer doing animated characters; others are best at announcing and narration, and there are those who can do both. This does not necessarily mean that one kind of voice talent is better than the other. The idea is to identify what style of voice(s) you really have.

The more you practice reading and performing using the *Voice Over Toolbox*, the more you'll discover the quality, style and range of your voice. Be ready and able to define your talents.

Here's a sample list to help you get started in choosing and describing your personal style:

Announcer	Authoritative, Warm, Friendly
Narrator	Rich, Smooth, Powerful, Bright
Real	Natural, Conversational
Characters	Hip, Cool, Flirty, Tough
Animation	Comical, Wacky, Spooky
Spokesperson	Hard/Soft Sell, Honest, Upbeat

There are many more attitudes and styles... Which ones describe yours?

CREATE YOUR OWN "VOICE OVER PALETTE"

When you read a script, draw from your personal list and begin to create your *Voice Over Palette.* Like a painter's palette, you'll put together a range of attitudes, colors and styles that accurately represents your unique *vocal personality.*

Begin by making a list of 5-10 word descriptions that capture and define your true self. There are endless combinations — just make it yours. For ideas, refer to the *Voice Over Toolbox.*

Know who you are and you'll be on the right path to defining your style, finding the *honey* and the *money* in your voice.

NEXT STEPS

If your goal is to become a professional voice over actor, in time, you'll need to:
- Record your voice demo.
- Put together a portable/home studio or have access to a professional studio.
- Explore getting an agent.
- Consider joining one or more online casting services.
- Network and develop a social media-marketing plan.
- Showcase your demo and attract clients to audition and hire you.

Whew! If all this seems like too much, don't worry. This is the big picture. You can choose to be on the fast track or take small steps at a time, when you're ready for it, and continue to set goals.

As you practice using the *Voice Over Toolbox*, keep track of your progress. If you plan to audition or record a voice over project; speak at a conference or special event; talk on the phone to clients and friends; prepare for an all important job interview; seek to increase sales, or just want to gain confidence in the way you communicate... I trust this guidebook offers countless ways to express your unique *vocal personality* and results in finding the power *and* the money in your voice!

Follow up with phone coaching, in-studio training, voice over demo and production services! Contact me at Radio Magic Studio for more information.

Madeleine Wild, M.A., Voice Director
www.radiomagic.com

SUCCESS STORIES

"I just woke up, remembering a vivid dream of auditioning for a voice-over job! It wasn't easy, I remember trying to get focused and thinking about how to approach the copy I was given... It seems I had all the 'tools' I needed in the dream, it was a matter of letting go of the self- consciousness and concentrating on the material. (I was thinking about different ways to say what I was given, and forgetting about the room full of other people surrounding me). Say, could some of this stuff from class actually be sinking in? What a concept!"
-Jean Lyon, Student

"To: Madeleine Wild
Subject: The perfect response!
Here is the e-mail I received this morning upon delivery of my demo to a voiceover agent in Atlanta. "Great Demo. Please call me." THANKS!!!"
-Lesley Hamilton Hill, Musical Theater Singer, Voice Talent

"I have to tell you, Madeleine...my skills as a voiceover talent definitely stand up to these fellow actors here today who have been working for 20 plus years in the business! Thank you for getting me prepared! You're the best!"
-Debbie Bowen, Voice Over Talent, Nail Artistry, Student

"Madeleine Wild at Radio Magic guided me to tell my story in my own voice: inspiring me to find my own rhythm, prodding me to become an actress, and cajoling me to be my best."
-Catherine Sevenau, Author and Voice, Behind These Doors

"It's true! Madeleine Wild captures lightening in a bottle routinely! Thanks for a wonderful ad and a great time. In just a few words you put me right into the spot I needed to be in to make "Sparky" come alive... It's amazing to hear the difference expert direction can bring to voices."
-George Webber, Radio Show Host, Performance Artist

"The best Bay Area voice over guide bar none!! A most extraordinary experience and the meticulousness of a diamond cutter!! Madeleine is a dream to collaborate with and a consummate professional."
-Kathleen Callan, Voice Over, Owner Chanteuse Designs

"Hi Madeleine, I just finished a voiceover project with Hello Collective. You always said that my money voice would be my "OM" and you were dead on. That was precisely the voice they wanted to hear. And because the project went so well they will be using me on future recordings. Big thanks."
-Nick Zane, Voice Over Talent, Student

"I wanted to let you know that my Voice Over with Walmart.com went great. Once again, the tools you've shared allowed me to walk into the session feeling confident and comfortable with the process. I was able to connect with the copy and make it come alive. It was a blast! More boundless gratitude to you!!!"
-Rob McCulloch, Voice Over Talent, Tonry Talent Agency

"In just one half hour you opened up what feels like a lifetime of blocked expression... It jazzed my creativity and confidence. Thank you from the bottom of my heart/voice."
-Jay Bird, Singer, Poet, Storyteller, Healer

INSPIRATION ON ACTING AND PERFORMING — FROM ACTORS, WRITERS AND DIRECTORS

"Acting is about becoming who you are." - Felicity Huffman, Academy Award winning film, stage and TV actress, best known as Lynette on Desperate Housewives.

"Life isn't about finding yourself. Life is about creating yourself." - George Bernard Shaw, Nobel Prize-winning playwright, essayist and critic.

"… On the stage truth is what the actor truly believes." *- Konstantin Stanislavski, A Russian Theater and Acting innovator, is the father of the Stanislavski Method of acting.*

"Take risks, don't play it too safe. Leave a tip." (Something personal that reflects the essence of you.) - Billy Crystal, writer, producer, comedian, film director and actor.

"Stop thinking so much! To really perform, you have to give yourself over to the fact that you don't know what you're creating until you are done." - Conan O'Brien, Emmy-winning TV personality and late-night talk/variety show host.

"An artist's greatest successes are not found in a single rave performance, but, instead, in the way he or she uses that experience to keep moving forward—to evolve, to learn, to work." - Uta Hagen, A German-born American actress and acting teacher. She taught at HB Studio, a well-known New York City acting school, and married its co-founder, Herbert Berghof.

"The actor's purpose is to create a believable character. He creates belief for the audience when he creates belief for himself." - Charles McGraw, Author, Acting is Believing.

GLOSSARY

Voice over The unseen person whose voice is used in radio, film TV, books, narrations, online and CD-interactive. The speaker's words are heard over a picture. The finished product is a *voice over* and the performer is a voice over actor.

Voice over
Voice-over
Voiceover
Voiceovers
Voice talent
Voice over artist
Voice actor
Voice. . . . . All spellings and terms are acceptable!

Attitude An acting method used to portray a character and express your style, point of view, or specific emotion. Your *attitude* can be happy, friendly, flirty, goofy, serious... it's your choice, or whatever you are asked to do by the director.

Cadence The flow and phrasing of the words in the copy. How the reading comes together with the breaks and beats that are placed between the words.

Character How the actor expresses a role. In portraying a person (or, animal, plant, inanimate object), the actor draws on the unique distinctive qualities of his/her subject and aims to reflect its true personality, in mind, body and feeling.

Copy The script or text of a commercial or narration piece that you read.

Demo A demonstration digital audio file (MP3 or WAV) or CD of your voice talent, which includes a sampling of your style, range and repertoire. It's advisable to do this only after you've trained, practiced, developed your creative and technical skills and feel confident, with a good sense of your talent abilities. This is a way to market your voice to agents, casting people and potential clients. The demo is usually 60-90 seconds in length and should be done professionally.

Focus Concentration on a specific theme, topic, character, attitude or emotion.

Hard sell Strong, aggressive tough approach to reading the copy.

Soft sell Relaxed, laid back approach to reading the copy.

Personal Signature Your voice is unique, like a personal signature. It has defining qualities, which make it truly yours alone.

Tags One-liner or two-line pieces of copy that describe a product, service or idea. It may stand alone, or can be featured at the beginning or end of a commercial or script.

One-Liners Similar to tags. Only these are usually one line only.

Tempo How slowly or quickly you read.

Timeframe Generally speaking, sponsors need to convey their commercial messages in 15, 30, or 60 seconds. The voice actor has to perform the commercial in that time effectively, clearly and believably.

Pitch High or low. Pitch represents the ups and downs of your voice. The musical level at which you speak.

Rhythm The cadence of your voice when you speak or read copy.

Timing A rhythm, a pace, a tempo. It refers to how slowly or quickly a person speaks in reading the copy or script.

Tone The sound quality of voice. The ups and downs one hears in normal conversation; the musical level at which a person speaks.

Pace The speed in which you choose to read the copy.

Volume Loud and soft. Raising or lowering the volume of your voice, changes the quality and varies your delivery. Bring it up/down to increase or decrease the intensity of your reading.

Directions and Common Phrases from Directors

Be real Make your character and style sincere, natural, believable and true to life as possible.

Make it flow Make your delivery smooth and complete. Avoid sounding "choppy."

Make it yours Personalize the copy you're reading and the character you're portraying.

Mark the copy Underline or highlight the written page to help guide you in choosing emphasis and timing. Decide which words you want to emphasize, where to pause or breathe, and mark "trouble" places.

More energy Just when you think you're putting it out there, the director may say, "more energy." Pick up your the delivery and put it out there with a little more conviction. Punch it up!

Romance the mic Make a friendly connection with the microphone. Feel comfortable with it and really *talk* to your listener. Let it show off your voice and personal sound in the best way.

Slate your name Before doing the take, say or record your name so that your voice can be identified as the actor doing the reading.

Take "Take one, take two, take three..." These phrases are commonly used in recording. Each time the *take* serves to identify the sequence of the actor's reads.

Talk to me "Make me believe it!" Don't just *read* it. Be conversational. This is what a Director may ask you to do in order to help make the copy come alive.

Throw it away When you're reading copy, don't *think* about it. Say it and read it naturally without any particular emphasis. Just let it go.

Warm up the copy Smile and we can hear it. Make your delivery friendly.

Pick-up In a recording session, your director may want you to repeat a line that had unwanted sounds, or may not have been emphasized or spoken correctly. A pick-up is a do-over, a redo or a retake in a recording session.

ABOUT MADELEINE WILD - "OH, THE PLACES I'VE BEEN."

I'm a voice director. My passion is working with actors, authors, businesses and dreamers! My purpose is to inspire people to find the power of their voices. I understand the world of possibility...

I grew up in the suburbs of New York City. I had one foot in education, as a college student and pre-school teacher, and the other as an actress, into *method acting*, drama and excitement. When I was 18, I moved to Greenwich Village. My first apartment was at 13 West 13th Street, next door to actress and free spirit, Margaret Corey, daughter of comedian Professor Irwin Corey. Irwin would take us to Johnny Carson's Tonight Show and introduce us to Johnny, as well as other comedians, stage and screen stars.

Relocating to Sausalito, California, I began my career in voice over as the original host and creator of *Hot Air*, a kids' radio show starring budding actor/comedian Robin Williams. Robin played a few wonderful characters on my kids' radio show. He created Mother Nature, Swami Sack-a-Bananas and Jazz Baby. Looking back, Robin Williams was someone who turned possibility into amazing success. He starred as Mork in the television series *Mork and Mindy* and the rest is history.

I moved to Los Angeles and became a Beverly Hills literary/talent agent, representing Peter Bergman (*The Firesign Theater*) and Disney voices Will Ryan and Phil Barron. Will is an Academy Award-winning voice talent today. Since 1991, I've settled in Sonoma, California, and own an established voice over studio that has trained hundreds of voice actors. I wrote my Master's Thesis on Voice Over and Language Arts, received a grant from The Grateful Dead Rex Foundation, and developed the *Voice Over Toolbox*, a theory-based training method. I hope my proven techniques provide the way to your voice over success!

Made in the USA
San Bernardino, CA
02 June 2018